FINDING BALANCE IN YOUR LIFE

STRATEGIES FOR ACHIEVING INNER PEACE

DR. JAGADEESH PILLAI

|| Dedicated to all wisdom seekers around the World ||

ॐ

Contents

Contents

PRAYER

**Saraswati Namasthubhyam Varade Kamarupini
Vidyarambham Karishyami Siddhir Bavathume Sadha**

Greetings to Devi Saraswati, the benevolent granter of
blessings and fulfiller of desires. O Devi, as I embark on my
studies, I humbly ask that you grant me the wisdom to
comprehend correctly.

About The Author

Dr. Jagadeesh Pillai is a renowned Guinness World Record holder, writer, and researcher hailing from Varanasi, also known as the abode of Lord Shiva. With a Ph.D. in Vedic Science and a range of creative ideas and achievements, he is a true polymath. He is the author of more than 100 books including Research Publications. Although his roots can be traced back to Kerala, the people of Varanasi hold him in high regard and affectionately consider him one of their own.

In 1998, Dr. Pillai was offered a job at Banaras Hindu University, but he left the position after only two months to pursue greater goals in life. He believed that in order to study Indian scriptures and engage in other creative endeavours, he needed to retire from the daily grind of working solely for money at a young age.

He started an export business from scratch, using the knowledge he had gained from a previous job in the industry. His intelligence and unique approach to business led to great success in a short period of time, earning him more in just a decade and a half than he would have in a lifetime working in a government job. Upon the passing of Dr. APJ Abdul Kalam, Dr. Pillai decided to leave the business and dedicate himself to reading, studying, researching, and experimenting.

During his tenure in the export business, Dr. Pillai traveled to over 16 countries, gaining valuable insight and experiencing the world and life in detail.

Dr. Pillai has achieved four Guinness World Records in the following subjects:

"Script to Screen" - In this record, Dr. Pillai produced and directed an animation film within the shortest time possible, breaking the previous record set by Canadians. He has also received numerous national and international awards and recognitions for this achievement.

Longest Line of Postcards - For this record, Dr. Pillai created a line of 16,300 postcards on the occasion of the 163rd anniversary of Indian Postal Day. The event also included a questionnaire about the Indian flag.

Largest Poster Awareness Campaign - Dr. Pillai designed an awareness campaign on the subject of "Beti Bachao - Beti Padhao" (Save the Girl Child - Educate the Girl Child) to achieve this record.

Largest Envelope - In tribute to the Indian Prime Minister's "Make in India" initiative, Dr. Pillai created a 4000 square meter envelope using waste paper to achieve this record.

Attempted - **70000 Candles on a 210 kg Cake** - To celebrate the 70th Indian Independence Day, Dr. Pillai attempted to light 70,000 candles on a 210 kg cake, which was recorded in World Records India.

Attempted - **Documentary on Dhamek Stupa of Sarnath in 17 Languages** - Dr. Pillai attempted to create a documentary on the Dhamek Stupa of Sarnath, dubbing it in 17 different languages. The result of this attempt is currently awaiting confirmation from the Guinness World Records.

Dr. Pillai is skilled in teaching the Bhagavad Gita, a Hindu scripture, and is popular among young people. He has helped many young people improve their lives through his motivational teachings.

In addition to teaching, he has composed and sung numerous Sanskrit Bhajans and patriotic songs.

He has also written and directed several short films and documentaries for awareness campaigns, and has volunteered with the police in both UP and Kerala to spread awareness about various issues through videos and photography.

Incredibly, he has produced and directed over 100 documentaries about the city of Varanasi, all on his own.

He has also helped and guided more than 25 boys and girls to achieve world records through creative and innovative methods. He is a multifaceted person who uses his intellect and the blessings given to him by God to excel in various areas. He is both a teacher and a student, always learning and teaching, and is able to master any subject he comes across.

He is a selfless social activist and motivational speaker who has overcome struggles and failures to become a successful and enthusiastic individual with a rich life experience.

In addition to his work with the Bhagavad Gita, he is also an efficient Tarot card reader, Astro-Vastu consultant, and a talented singer and composer. He has sung the entire Ram Charita Manas and Bhagavad Gita in his own compositions, and has sung the phrase "Lokah Samastha Sukhino Bhavantu" in 50 different languages. He is currently working on a detailed and scientific study of Vedas, Upanishads, Puranas, and the Bhagavad Gita. He has also composed and sung the Hanuman Chalisa and Gayatri Mantra in 108 and 1008 different compositions, respectively.

Awards - Four Times Guinness World Records, Winner of Mahatma Gandhi Vishwa Shanti Puraskar, Mahatma Gandhi Global Peace Ambassador, Kashi Ratna Award, Dr. APJ Abdul Kalam Motivational Person of the Year 2017, Mother Teresa Award, Indira Gandhi Priyadarshini Award, Bharat Vikas Ratna Award, Udyog Ratna Award, Vigyan Prasar Award, Poorvanchal Ratn Samman.

PREFACE

In Finding Balance in Your Life: Strategies for Achieving Inner Peace, readers will discover a comprehensive guide to achieving inner peace and balance in their lives. Through a combination of practical advice, personal anecdotes, and inspiring stories, this book provides readers with the tools they need to create a life of balance and harmony.

The book begins by exploring the concept of balance and how it can be achieved. It then delves into the various strategies that can be used to achieve inner peace, such as mindfulness, meditation, and self-care. Readers will learn how to create a balanced lifestyle that works for them, and how to maintain it over time.

The book also provides readers with the opportunity to reflect on their own lives and how they can make changes to create a more balanced life. It encourages readers to take a holistic approach to their lives, and to consider all aspects of their lives, including their physical, mental, and emotional health.

Finding Balance in Your Life: Strategies for Achieving Inner Peace is an invaluable resource for anyone looking to create a life of balance and harmony. It is a must-read for anyone seeking to create a life of inner peace and balance. With its practical advice, inspiring stories, and personal anecdotes, this book is sure to provide readers with the tools they need to create a life of balance and harmony.

I

Introduction: Finding Balance in Life

Life is a constantly evolving journey that presents us with a wide range of challenges and opportunities. We often find ourselves torn between competing demands, struggling to maintain a healthy work-life balance, and trying to find meaning and purpose in our daily activities. In a world that is fast-paced and always on the go, finding balance can seem like an elusive goal.

But what exactly is balance?

In its simplest form, balance is the state of being evenly distributed or in proportion. When we talk about finding balance in life, we are referring to the process of creating a harmonious relationship between all of the various elements of our lives. This includes work, relationships, personal growth, health and well-being, and leisure time.

Finding balance in life is important for several reasons.

For one, when we feel balanced, we are able to live a more fulfilling life. We are able to connect with others in meaningful ways, pursue our passions and interests, and feel a sense of accomplishment and satisfaction. Additionally, when we are balanced, we are better equipped to handle the challenges that life throws our way. We are able to approach problems with a sense of calm and resilience, and we are more likely to make informed decisions that benefit us and those around us.

So, how do we find balance in our lives?

The process of finding balance is different for everyone, but there are some common strategies and approaches that can help. The first step is to take a good look at your life and assess where you are currently at. What are your priorities? What are your values? What do you want to achieve? By answering these questions, you can begin to create a roadmap for the future and set realistic goals for yourself.

Another important aspect of finding balance is self-care.

This includes taking care of your physical health, emotional well-being, and mental health. This can include regular exercise, healthy eating, getting enough sleep, and engaging in activities that bring you joy and relaxation. It is important to prioritize self-care and make it a non-negotiable part of your daily routine.

Time management is another key component of finding balance.

This means setting realistic boundaries and learning to say no to activities or commitments that are not aligned with your values and goals. It also means prioritizing your time and focusing on the activities and relationships that matter most to you.

Mindfulness and self-awareness are also essential components of finding balance.

Mindfulness involves being present in the moment and focusing on your thoughts and feelings without judgment. Self-awareness involves understanding your own emotions and motivations, and taking responsibility for your actions and decisions.

In conclusion, finding balance in life is a journey that requires effort, patience, and self-reflection. It involves creating a harmonious relationship between all of the various elements of your life, and making sure that your daily activities reflect your values, priorities, and goals. By taking the time to focus on self-care, time management, mindfulness, and self-awareness, you can begin to find the balance that you need to live a happy, healthy, and fulfilling life.

"The key to finding balance in life is to prioritize what matters most and let go of the rest."

ଔ

II

Understanding Your Needs and Priorities

In order to lead a balanced and fulfilling life, it is important to understand your own needs and priorities. This means taking the time to reflect on what truly matters to you, what gives you a sense of purpose and meaning, and what makes you feel happy and content. By identifying and prioritizing your needs, you can create a roadmap for your life that aligns with your values and allows you to pursue your goals with greater focus and clarity.

The first step in understanding your needs and priorities is to engage in self-reflection. This can be done through journaling, meditating, or simply taking a walk in nature. During this time, ask yourself questions like: What do I value most in life? What brings me joy and satisfaction? What do I want to achieve in the next year, 5 years, or 10 years? What are my non-negotiables – things that I simply cannot do without?

Once you have a clearer sense of what you want and need, it is time to prioritize. This means organizing your goals and desires into categories based on their importance. For example, your health and wellbeing might be your top priority, followed by your relationships with loved ones, your career, and other interests.

It is important to remember that your needs and priorities can change over time. As you grow and evolve, you may find that certain things that once mattered to you no longer hold the same level of significance, while others take on greater importance. It is okay to re-evaluate your priorities and make changes as needed – this is a natural part of the growth and self-discovery process.

One way to keep your needs and priorities front and center is to make a written list and refer to it regularly. Seeing your priorities in writing can help to solidify them in your mind and keep you on track. You might also consider incorporating them into your daily routine by setting aside time each day to work on your priorities or to reflect on what is most important to you.

In conclusion, understanding your needs and priorities is a critical step in finding balance in your life. By knowing what matters most to you, you can make choices that align with your values and goals, leading to greater satisfaction and happiness. Remember to be patient and kind to yourself as you embark on this journey, and trust that by putting your needs and priorities first, you are taking a positive step towards creating the life you want.

"The secret to inner peace is to accept the things you cannot change and have the courage to change the things you can."

III

Setting Boundaries and Limits

In order to find balance in your life, it is essential to establish clear boundaries and limits. Boundaries help to protect your time, energy, and mental space, allowing you to prioritize your needs and focus on what is most important to you. By setting boundaries, you are able to maintain control over your life and make choices that support your wellbeing and happiness.

One of the first steps in setting boundaries is to identify what needs to be protected. This might include your time, your relationships, your personal space, or your work. Once you have a clear understanding of what you want to protect, you can start to set limits around it.

One effective way to set boundaries is to be clear and direct with the people in your life. For example, if you need to prioritize your work, you might tell a friend or family member that you cannot take phone calls or answer emails during certain hours of the day. If you need to protect your personal space, you might establish a rule that you do not discuss personal matters at work.

Another important aspect of setting boundaries is to be firm and consistent. It can be tempting to bend the rules or make exceptions for certain people or situations, but this can undermine the effectiveness of your boundaries and lead to feelings of resentment or frustration. Instead, it is important to be clear and consistent in your approach, so that others understand what you expect from them and what you are willing to tolerate.

It is also important to be compassionate and understanding towards yourself. Setting boundaries can be challenging, especially if you are used to putting others first. However, it is important to remember that taking care of yourself is not selfish – it is a necessary step in finding balance and happiness in your life.

In conclusion, setting boundaries and limits is a crucial aspect of finding balance in your life. By establishing clear rules around what you will and will not tolerate, you can take control over your time, energy, and mental space, allowing you to prioritize your needs and focus on what is most important to you. With patience, compassion, and a commitment to consistency, you can learn to set effective boundaries and take a positive step towards finding inner peace and balance.

"The journey to balance begins with self-awareness and ends with self-mastery."

ജ

IV

Prioritizing Self-Care

In order to find balance and inner peace in your life, it is essential to prioritize self-care. Self-care refers to the deliberate actions and habits we engage in to maintain our physical, mental, and emotional wellbeing. By taking care of ourselves, we are better equipped to tackle life's challenges and to find meaning and purpose in our lives.

Self-care can take many forms, ranging from physical activities like exercise or yoga, to mental and emotional practices like therapy or mindfulness meditation. What is important is that the activities you engage in support your overall wellbeing and align with your needs and priorities.

One key aspect of prioritizing self-care is to make it a non-negotiable part of your routine. This means setting aside time each day, or each week, to engage in self-care activities, even when life gets busy or stressful. By making self-care a priority, you are sending a message to yourself and to others that taking care of yourself is important and valuable.

It is also important to experiment and find what works best for you. Self-care is a personal journey, and what works for one person may not work for another. It is important to be open to trying new things, and to find what activities bring you the most peace, joy, and fulfillment.

It is important to be compassionate and forgiving towards yourself as you engage in self-care. Sometimes, life can get in the way and you may not be able to prioritize self-care as much as you would like. It is important to remember that self-care is a process, and that it is okay to make mistakes and to have off days. The most important thing is to keep trying and to maintain a positive attitude towards your self-care journey.

In conclusion, prioritizing self-care is a critical step in finding balance and inner peace in your life. By taking care of your physical, mental, and emotional wellbeing, you are better equipped to handle life's challenges and to find meaning and purpose in your life. With a commitment to making self-care a non-negotiable part of your routine, and a willingness to experiment and find what works best for you, you can take a positive step towards a more balanced and fulfilling life.

"The path to inner peace is paved with small, consistent steps towards balance."

౭౦

V

Creating a Support System

One of the key strategies for finding balance and inner peace in your life is to create a support system. A support system is a network of individuals who provide you with emotional, mental, and practical support. Having a support system can help you to feel less isolated and more connected, and can provide you with the encouragement and motivation you need to achieve your goals.

One of the first steps in creating a support system is to identify the people in your life who you trust and who you feel comfortable talking to about your thoughts and feelings. This might include family members, friends, coworkers, or a support group. It is important to choose individuals who are supportive, non-judgmental, and who you feel comfortable confiding in.

It is also important to be proactive in building and

maintaining your support system. This might involve reaching out to individuals who you would like to have in your support system, or participating in activities and events that bring you into contact with like-minded individuals. It is important to communicate your needs and to be open and receptive to the support of others.

Another aspect of creating a support system is to seek professional support when needed. This might involve seeing a therapist, a coach, or a counselor. Professional support can provide you with the tools and strategies you need to navigate life's challenges and to find balance and inner peace.

It is important to remember that a support system is not a one-way street. You should also be willing to support others, to listen and to offer encouragement and motivation when needed. By being a supportive member of your community, you can help to build stronger and more meaningful relationships, and to find deeper levels of connection and fulfillment.

In conclusion, creating a support system is a key strategy for finding balance and inner peace in your life. By surrounding yourself with individuals who provide you with emotional, mental, and practical support, you can feel less isolated, more connected, and better equipped to handle life's challenges. With a commitment to building and maintaining strong and supportive relationships, you can take a positive step towards a more balanced and fulfilling life.

♋

"The only way to achieve true balance in life
is to be mindful of your thoughts, words, and
actions."

છ

VI

Mindful Practices for Stress Reduction

Stress is a natural and unavoidable part of life, and can have a significant impact on our physical, mental, and emotional wellbeing. In order to find balance and inner peace, it is essential to find effective ways to manage and reduce stress. Mindful practices can be a powerful tool in reducing stress, and in improving our overall wellbeing.

Mindful practices are activities that involve bringing our attention to the present moment, and to our physical, mental, and emotional experiences. This might involve practices like mindfulness meditation, deep breathing, or yoga. The goal of these practices is to cultivate a sense of awareness and presence, and to reduce stress and anxiety by calming the mind and the body.

One of the key benefits of mindful practices is that they can help to reduce stress and anxiety by shifting our focus away from our worries and concerns, and towards the present moment. By bringing our attention to our breath and to our physical sensations, we can calm the mind and the body, and reduce feelings of stress and anxiety.

Mindful practices can also help us to develop a greater sense of self-awareness, and to understand the ways in which our thoughts and emotions impact our wellbeing. This can help us to identify and manage stressors more effectively, and to find more effective and healthy ways of coping with stress.

It is important to start with small and manageable practices, and to find a practice that works best for you. Mindful practices can be challenging at first, but with time and practice, they can become a powerful tool for reducing stress and for improving our overall wellbeing.

In conclusion, mindful practices can be a powerful tool for reducing stress and for improving our overall wellbeing. By bringing our attention to the present moment, and to our physical, mental, and emotional experiences, we can reduce stress and anxiety, and cultivate a greater sense of awareness and presence. With a commitment to incorporating mindful practices into your daily routine, you can take a positive step towards finding balance and inner peace in your life.

"The key to finding balance is to focus on the present moment and let go of the past and future."

ॐ

VII

Finding Balance Between Work and Play

Finding balance between work and play is a common challenge for many people, and can have a significant impact on our physical, mental, and emotional wellbeing. The demands of work can often leave us feeling stressed, exhausted, and with little time or energy for the things that bring us joy and fulfillment. In order to find balance and inner peace, it is essential to find a healthy balance between work and play.

One of the key strategies for finding balance between work and play is to set clear boundaries and limits. This might involve setting specific work hours, or creating a schedule that allows for dedicated time for rest, recreation, and self-care. By setting these boundaries, you can ensure that you have the time and energy to pursue the things that bring you joy and fulfillment, and to recharge and refresh your mind and body.

Another strategy for finding balance between work and play is to prioritize self-care. This might involve engaging in physical exercise, practicing mindfulness, or participating in activities that bring you joy and fulfillment. By taking care of your physical, mental, and emotional needs, you can ensure that you are better equipped to handle the demands of work, and to find a healthy balance between work and play.

It is also important to communicate your needs and boundaries with those around you. This might involve setting clear expectations with coworkers and family members, or sharing your schedule with friends and loved ones. By communicating your needs, you can ensure that those around you are aware of your boundaries and are better equipped to support you.

In conclusion, finding balance between work and play is a critical component of finding balance and inner peace in your life. By setting clear boundaries and limits, prioritizing self-care, and communicating your needs, you can ensure that you have the time and energy to pursue the things that bring you joy and fulfillment, and to recharge and refresh your mind and body. With a commitment to finding a healthy balance between work and play, you can take a positive step towards a more balanced and fulfilling life.

"The best way to achieve inner peace is to practice gratitude and be thankful for all that you have."

&

VIII
Nourishing Body and Soul

Nourishing both the body and the soul is an essential part of finding balance and inner peace in your life. Our physical, mental, and emotional wellbeing are all interconnected, and it is important to take care of all aspects of our health in order to achieve balance and wellbeing.

One of the key ways to nourish both the body and the soul is to make healthy food choices. A balanced and nutritious diet can provide the vitamins, minerals, and nutrients needed to support our physical health, and can also help to boost our mood and energy levels. In addition to making healthy food choices, it is also important to stay hydrated, and to limit the amount of caffeine, alcohol, and processed foods in our diets.

Another important aspect of nourishing the body and the

soul is to engage in regular physical activity. Physical activity can help to boost our energy levels, improve our mood, and support our overall physical health. Whether it is through participating in a sport, going for a walk, or practicing yoga, it is important to find an activity that you enjoy and that you can incorporate into your daily routine.

In addition to taking care of our physical health, it is also important to nourish our souls by engaging in activities that bring us joy and fulfillment. This might involve participating in a hobby, spending time with loved ones, or pursuing a creative endeavor. By engaging in activities that bring us joy and fulfillment, we can nourish our souls and find greater balance and inner peace in our lives.

It is also important to make time for self-reflection and introspection. This might involve keeping a journal, meditating, or engaging in other contemplative practices. By taking time to reflect on our thoughts, feelings, and experiences, we can gain a deeper understanding of our needs and priorities, and can take steps to find greater balance and inner peace in our lives.

In conclusion, nourishing both the body and the soul is a critical component of finding balance and inner peace in your life. By making healthy food choices, engaging in regular physical activity, pursuing activities that bring us joy and fulfillment, and making time for self-reflection and introspection, we can support our overall health and wellbeing, and find greater balance and inner peace in our lives.

୫

"The only way to find balance in life is to make time for yourself and your passions."

ॐ

IX

Making Time for Relaxation

In today's fast-paced world, it can be all too easy to become overwhelmed and stressed. This is why it is so important to make time for relaxation in your life, in order to find balance and inner peace. By taking the time to unwind and recharge, you can reduce stress and anxiety, and promote overall wellbeing.

One of the key ways to make time for relaxation is to incorporate it into your daily routine. This might involve taking a few minutes each day to meditate, engage in deep breathing exercises, or simply to sit quietly and reflect. By making relaxation a regular part of your routine, you can create a sense of calm and peace in your life, even amidst the chaos and stress of daily life.

In addition to incorporating relaxation into your daily routine, it is also important to make time for leisure activities that bring you joy and fulfillment. This might involve spending time with loved ones, engaging in a hobby, or simply taking a walk in nature. By engaging in activities that bring you joy and fulfillment, you can promote relaxation, reduce stress, and find greater balance and inner peace in your life.

Another effective way to promote relaxation is to engage in mindfulness practices. This might involve practicing yoga, engaging in tai chi, or simply focusing on your breathing. Mindfulness practices can help you to become more aware of your thoughts and feelings, and can help you to develop a sense of calm and inner peace, even in the midst of stressful or chaotic situations.

Finally, it is important to make time for rest and sleep. Our bodies and minds need time to recharge, and sleep is one of the most effective ways to promote relaxation and wellbeing. By making sure to get enough sleep each night, you can reduce stress and anxiety, and promote overall wellbeing.

In conclusion, making time for relaxation is an essential part of finding balance and inner peace in your life. By incorporating relaxation into your daily routine, engaging in leisure activities that bring you joy and fulfillment, practicing mindfulness, and making time for rest and sleep, you can reduce stress and anxiety, promote relaxation, and find greater balance and inner peace in your life.

"The key to achieving balance is to be
mindful of your thoughts, feelings, and
emotions."

ॐ

X

Cultivating Healthy Habits

Healthy habits are key to achieving balance and inner peace in your life. By cultivating healthy habits, you can reduce stress, improve physical and mental wellbeing, and promote overall balance and happiness.

One of the most important healthy habits to cultivate is regular exercise. Exercise has been shown to reduce stress and anxiety, improve mood, and promote overall physical and mental health. Whether it's a daily walk, a yoga class, or a vigorous workout, incorporating exercise into your daily routine can have a profound impact on your wellbeing.

Another important healthy habit to cultivate is eating a balanced diet. A healthy diet that includes plenty of fruits and vegetables, lean protein, and whole grains can provide your body with the essential nutrients it needs to function optimally. Additionally, eating a balanced diet can help you maintain a healthy weight, reduce stress and anxiety, and promote overall wellbeing.

In addition to exercise and a healthy diet, it is also important to cultivate habits that promote relaxation and stress reduction. This might involve practicing mindfulness, engaging in deep breathing exercises, or simply taking a few minutes each day to simply sit quietly and reflect. By taking the time to unwind and reduce stress, you can promote relaxation, reduce anxiety, and find greater balance and inner peace in your life.

Another important healthy habit to cultivate is making time for sleep. Sleep is essential for physical and mental health, and by making sure to get enough sleep each night, you can reduce stress, improve mood, and promote overall wellbeing.

Finally, it is important to cultivate healthy habits in your relationships. This might involve setting boundaries and limits, engaging in open and honest communication, and spending quality time with loved ones. By nurturing your relationships, you can promote greater balance and inner peace in your life.

In conclusion, cultivating healthy habits is an essential part of finding balance and inner peace in your life. Whether it's exercise, a balanced diet, mindfulness practices, sleep, or healthy relationships, taking steps to cultivate healthy habits can have a profound impact on your wellbeing, and can help you to find greater balance and inner peace in your life.

&

"The path to inner peace is to be kind to
yourself and to others."

XI

Practicing Compassion and Kindness

Compassion and kindness are essential elements in finding balance and inner peace in your life. By cultivating compassion and kindness in your daily life, you can promote greater happiness, reduce stress, and foster deeper and more meaningful relationships with others.

One way to practice compassion and kindness is to engage in acts of service and volunteer work. Whether it's donating your time to a local charity or simply helping a neighbor in need, practicing acts of kindness and compassion can have a profound impact on your own wellbeing and the wellbeing of those around you.

Another way to cultivate compassion and kindness is through mindfulness and self-reflection. By taking time to reflect on your own thoughts, feelings, and actions, you can gain a greater understanding of yourself and the ways in which you interact with others. This self-awareness can help you to cultivate greater compassion and kindness in your daily life.

In addition, it is important to practice compassion and kindness in your relationships with others. This might involve engaging in open and honest communication, showing empathy and understanding towards others, and offering support and encouragement when it is needed. By cultivating compassion and kindness in your relationships, you can foster deeper connections and find greater balance and inner peace in your life.

It is also important to practice compassion and kindness towards yourself. This might involve engaging in self-care practices, such as exercise and healthy eating, and taking time to relax and unwind. By being kind and compassionate towards yourself, you can reduce stress, improve your overall wellbeing, and find greater balance and inner peace in your life.

In conclusion, practicing compassion and kindness is an essential part of finding balance and inner peace in your life. Whether it's through acts of service, mindfulness and self-reflection, or cultivating compassion and kindness in your relationships, taking steps to cultivate compassion and kindness in your daily life can have a profound impact on your wellbeing, and can help you to find greater balance and inner peace in your life.

ॐ

"The secret to finding balance is to be flexible
and open to change."

XII

Making Room for Changes

Change is an inevitable part of life, and making room for changes can be a key factor in finding balance and inner peace. By embracing change and adapting to new circumstances, you can grow and evolve, and discover new opportunities for happiness and fulfillment.

One way to make room for changes is to cultivate a growth mindset. This involves embracing challenges and viewing failures as opportunities for growth and learning, rather than as setbacks or defeat. With a growth mindset, you can face changes with resilience, determination, and a positive outlook, and find greater balance and inner peace in your life.

It's also important to practice self-reflection and self-awareness. By taking time to reflect on your thoughts, feelings, and actions, you can gain a better understanding of yourself, and identify areas where changes may be necessary. This can help you to make room for changes in your life, and find greater balance and inner peace.

In addition, it is important to be open to new experiences and to seek out new opportunities. Whether it's taking up a new hobby, exploring new places, or trying new foods, being open to new experiences can help you to grow and evolve, and find greater balance and inner peace in your life.

It's also important to cultivate strong relationships and to seek out support when changes occur. Whether it's through friends, family, or a support group, having a strong network of support can help you to navigate changes with greater ease and resilience, and find greater balance and inner peace in your life.

Finally, it is important to be flexible and to embrace change, even when it may be difficult. Whether it's adapting to new circumstances, letting go of old habits, or adjusting your priorities, embracing change and being flexible can help you to find greater balance and inner peace in your life.

In conclusion, making room for changes is an important part of finding balance and inner peace in your life. By cultivating a growth mindset, practicing self-reflection, being open to new experiences, seeking out support, and embracing change, you can find greater balance and inner peace, and grow and evolve in new and exciting ways.

જી

"The journey to inner peace begins with self-love and ends with self-acceptance."

ॐ

XIII

Letting Go of Excessive Responsibility

Taking on too much responsibility can be a common source of stress and imbalance in our lives. Whether it's taking on too many work responsibilities, caring for too many people, or assuming too much responsibility for things that are beyond our control, excessive responsibility can leave us feeling overwhelmed, stressed, and out of balance.

One key to finding balance and inner peace is to learn to let go of excessive responsibility. This involves recognizing when you are taking on too much and making deliberate choices about which responsibilities you want to keep and which you want to release.

One way to start letting go of excessive responsibility is to identify your core values and priorities. What is most important to you? What do you want to focus your time and energy on? By focusing on your core values and priorities, you can make more deliberate choices about which responsibilities you want to take on and which you want to let go.

Another way to let go of excessive responsibility is to set boundaries. This means learning to say "no" when you need to, and protecting your time and energy from the demands of others. It also means recognizing your own limitations and accepting that there are some things you simply cannot control.

It's also important to seek out support and to delegate responsibilities when necessary. Whether it's seeking help from a friend, a family member, or a professional, having a strong support system can help you to shoulder the weight of excessive responsibility and find greater balance and inner peace in your life.

In addition, it is important to practice self-care and to prioritize your own well-being. This means taking care of your physical, emotional, and mental health, and making time for activities and experiences that bring you joy and fulfillment. By prioritizing your own well-being, you can reduce stress, improve your resilience, and find greater balance and inner peace in your life.

Finally, it is important to cultivate a sense of gratitude and to focus on the things that bring you joy and fulfillment. By focusing on the things you are grateful for, you can let go of excessive responsibility, find greater balance and inner peace in your life, and enjoy the present moment.

In conclusion, letting go of excessive responsibility is an important part of finding balance and inner peace in your life. By identifying your core values and priorities, setting boundaries, seeking support, practicing self-care, and cultivating gratitude, you can reduce stress, improve your resilience, and find greater balance and inner peace in your life.

"The only way to achieve balance in life is to be mindful of your priorities and stay true to them."

ॐ

XIV

Celebrating Life's Milestones

Life is full of milestones, from big accomplishments to small victories. These milestones represent the progress we have made and the growth we have experienced over time. Celebrating these milestones can help us to recognize and appreciate our journey, and to find balance and inner peace in our lives.

One of the most important things to remember when celebrating life's milestones is to take the time to acknowledge them. This might mean taking a moment to reflect on what you have accomplished, or to celebrate with friends and loved ones. Whatever form it takes, taking the time to acknowledge your milestones can help you to recognize your progress and to feel more connected to your life journey.

Another key to celebrating life's milestones is to celebrate both the big and small victories. Whether it's landing a new job, completing a project, or simply making it through a tough day, it's important to acknowledge and celebrate your accomplishments, no matter how small they may seem. By doing so, you can build momentum and feel more motivated to continue making progress.

In addition, it is important to focus on what you have learned along the way. Every milestone provides an opportunity for growth and self-reflection. By taking the time to reflect on what you have learned, you can build your wisdom and grow as a person, which can lead to greater balance and inner peace in your life.

Another way to celebrate life's milestones is to find joy in the journey. This means focusing on the experience of growing and changing, rather than solely on the outcome. By finding joy in the journey, you can stay motivated and enjoy the process of growth, which can lead to greater balance and inner peace in your life.

Finally, it is important to be grateful for the journey and to recognize the people who have helped you along the way. Whether it's friends, family, or colleagues, taking the time to acknowledge the people who have supported you can help you to feel more connected and to find greater balance and inner peace in your life.

In conclusion, celebrating life's milestones is an important part of finding balance and inner peace in your life. By taking the time to acknowledge your accomplishments, focusing on what you have learned, finding joy in the journey, and being grateful for the journey and the people who have helped you along the way, you can recognize your progress, feel more motivated, and find greater balance and inner peace in your life.

"The key to finding balance is to take time to
appreciate the small moments and be present
in them."

ೞ

XV

Living in Harmony with the World

In order to achieve inner peace, it is important to cultivate a sense of harmony and balance in all aspects of our lives, including our relationship with the world around us. This means recognizing our interconnectedness with others, appreciating the natural environment, and finding ways to contribute to the greater good.

One way to live in harmony with the world is to practice mindfulness. This means being present in the moment and being aware of our thoughts, feelings, and sensations. By paying attention to the present moment, we can cultivate a deeper appreciation for life and the world around us. This can help to reduce stress and increase feelings of contentment and happiness.

Another way to live in harmony with the world is to engage in acts of kindness and generosity. This could involve volunteering your time or resources to help those in need, or simply performing small acts of kindness for those around you. By making a positive impact on the world, we can contribute to the greater good and experience a sense of purpose and fulfillment.

In addition to mindfulness and acts of kindness, it is also important to be mindful of our impact on the environment. This could involve reducing our carbon footprint, recycling, and conserving resources. By taking steps to care for the natural world, we can create a sense of balance and help to preserve the planet for future generations.

Lastly, it is important to cultivate a sense of gratitude and appreciation for the world around us. This could involve taking time each day to reflect on the things in your life that you are thankful for, or simply taking a moment to appreciate the beauty of nature. By cultivating a sense of gratitude and appreciation, we can create a deeper connection with the world and experience a greater sense of inner peace.

In conclusion, living in harmony with the world involves cultivating mindfulness, performing acts of kindness and generosity, being mindful of our impact on the environment, and cultivating a sense of gratitude and appreciation. By doing so, we can create a sense of balance in our lives and achieve a greater sense of inner peace.

"The path to inner peace is to be kind to
yourself and to forgive yourself for your
mistakes."

৪৩

OTHER BOOKS OF THE AUTHOR

1. The Moments When I Met God
2. Kashiyile Theertha Pathangal
3. Guru Gyan Vani
4. Abhiprerak Gita
5. Assi Se Jain Ghat Tak
6. Hopelessness of Arjuna
7. The Soul and It's True Nature
8. Sense of Action (Karma)
9. Action Through Wisdom
10. Action Through Wisdom
11. Theory And Practical of Every Action
12. Logical Understanding of The Supreme
13. The Imperishable Supreme
14. Yatra Nishadraj Se Hanuman Ghat Tak
15. Yatra Karnatak Ghat Se Raja Ghat Tak
16. Yatra Pandey Ghat Se Prayagraj Ghat Tak
17. Yatra Ranjendra Prasad Ghat Se Dattatreya Ghat Tak
18. Yaatrasindhiya Ghat Se Gwaliar Ghat Tak
19. Yatra Mangala Gauri Ghat Se Hanuman Gadhi Ghat Tak
20. Yatra Gaay Ghat Se Nishad Ghat Tak
21. Maa Ganga, Ghaten Evm Utsav
22. Ganga Arti Dev Deepavali Evam Any Utsav
23. Potentials of Digitalized India
24. Vedic Consciousness
25. A Brief Introduction to Vedic Science
26. Kashi Ke Barah Jyotirling
27. Impact Of Motivation
28. Let's Have a Milky Way Journey
29. Color Therapy in A Nutshell

30. Rigveda In a Nutshell
31. Yajurveda In a Nutshell
32. Samveda In a Nutshell
33. Atharva Veda In a Nutshell
34. Ayushman Bhava - Ayurveda
35. Srimad Bhagavad Gita and Upanishad Connection
36. Srimad Bhagavad Gita - An Attempt to Summarize Each Chapter.
37. Facts And Impact of Nakshatra
38. Astro Gems - Navaratna
39. Ekadashi - A Concise Overview
40. A Concise View of Hanuman Chalisa
41. Inspirational Gita
42. Nakshatraranyam
43. Summary of 18 Mahapuranas
44. Synopsis of 18 Upa Puranas
45. Rigvediya Upanishads
46. Shukla Yajurvediya Upanishads
47. Krishna Yajurvediya Upanishads
48. Samavediya Upanishads
49. Atharvavediya Upanishads
50. The Seven Great Sages
51. From Rocket Scientist to President Dr. Apj Abdul Kalam
52. The Visionary's Voice - Quotes of Dr. Apj Abdul Kalam
53. The Wisdom tf Swami Vivekananda: Insights and Inspiration from A Legendary Spiritual Teacher
54. Ayurvedic Remedies from The Garden
55. Sages and Seers
56. Rising Strong – Motivational Stories of Women
57. Beyond Flames -Mystery Stories of Funeral Ghat Manikarnika
58. The Origins of Tulsi: A Look at The Mythological Roots of The Plant"

CONTACT

DR. JAGADEESH PILLAI

MBA & PhD in Vedic Science

Four Times Guinness World Record Holder

Winner of Mahatma Gandhi Vishwa Shanti Puraskar and
Global Peace Ambassador

Gemology, Astro & Vastu Consultant - Spiritual Counselor

Consultant for designing World Record Ideas

Efficient Tarot Card Reader

9839093003

myrichindia@gmail.com

drjagadeeshpillai@facebook

drjagadeeshpillai@instagram

jagadeeshpillai@youtube

www. JAGADEESHPILLAI.com

|| LOKAHA SAMASTHAHA SUKHINO BHAVANTU ||